To my little monkey.
MAY YOU ALWAYS FIND THE INNER MAGIC INSIDE OF YOU AND NEVER LET ANYONE DULL YOUR INNER SHINE.
love mommy

Elizabeth Turunen is creative director, art director, writer, illustrator, surface designer, and chief coffee cup washer of her own business. Originally from Upper Michigan, Elizabeth now lives in Wisconsin with her beautiful daughter and very energetic puppy. Her dream is to use her talent in art and writing to inspire others to be comfortable with themselves and find the true magic within. By creating, LUNCH BOX HERO, "Using Your Inner Magic," Elizabeth is launching a mission in the hearts of heroes everywhere.

This is the first book in Elizabeth's anti-bullying and personal empowerment series. It plays an important role in her Lunch Box Hero campaign. Lunch Box Hero's mission is to build an anti-bullying squad of individuals who encourage empowerment through the use of imagination and "inner magic," helping transform negative feelings into positive ones. Our squad will help provide tools for students, schools, parents, and teachers to live out our mission of being yourself when the world gets tough. We will do this by embracing the hero within ourselves and each other through sharing acts of kindness, love, and respect.

To learn more about Lunch Box Hero and how you can join our squad, please visit gogravitate.com

No part of this publication may be reproduced, stored in a retrieval system, or transmitted in any form or by any means, electronic, mechanical, photocopying, recording, or otherwise, without the prior written permission of the copyright owner. For more information regarding permission, contact Gravitate Design LLC.

ISBN10: 1-986390-91-8
ISBN13: 978-1-986390-91-0

Text and illustrations copyright © 2018 by Elizabeth Turunen. All rights reserved.

Published by Gravitate Design LLC.
Green Bay, Wisconsin (USA)

Lunch Box Hero
using your INNER MAGIC

written & illustrated by Elizabeth Turunen

Today was the day!

Makayla sat **nervously**, her head low, as she watched her little brother, Jaxtin, slurp up his last bit of spilled milk from the table.

He looked like a thirsty lion soaking up the last drop of water in the hot Sahara Desert.

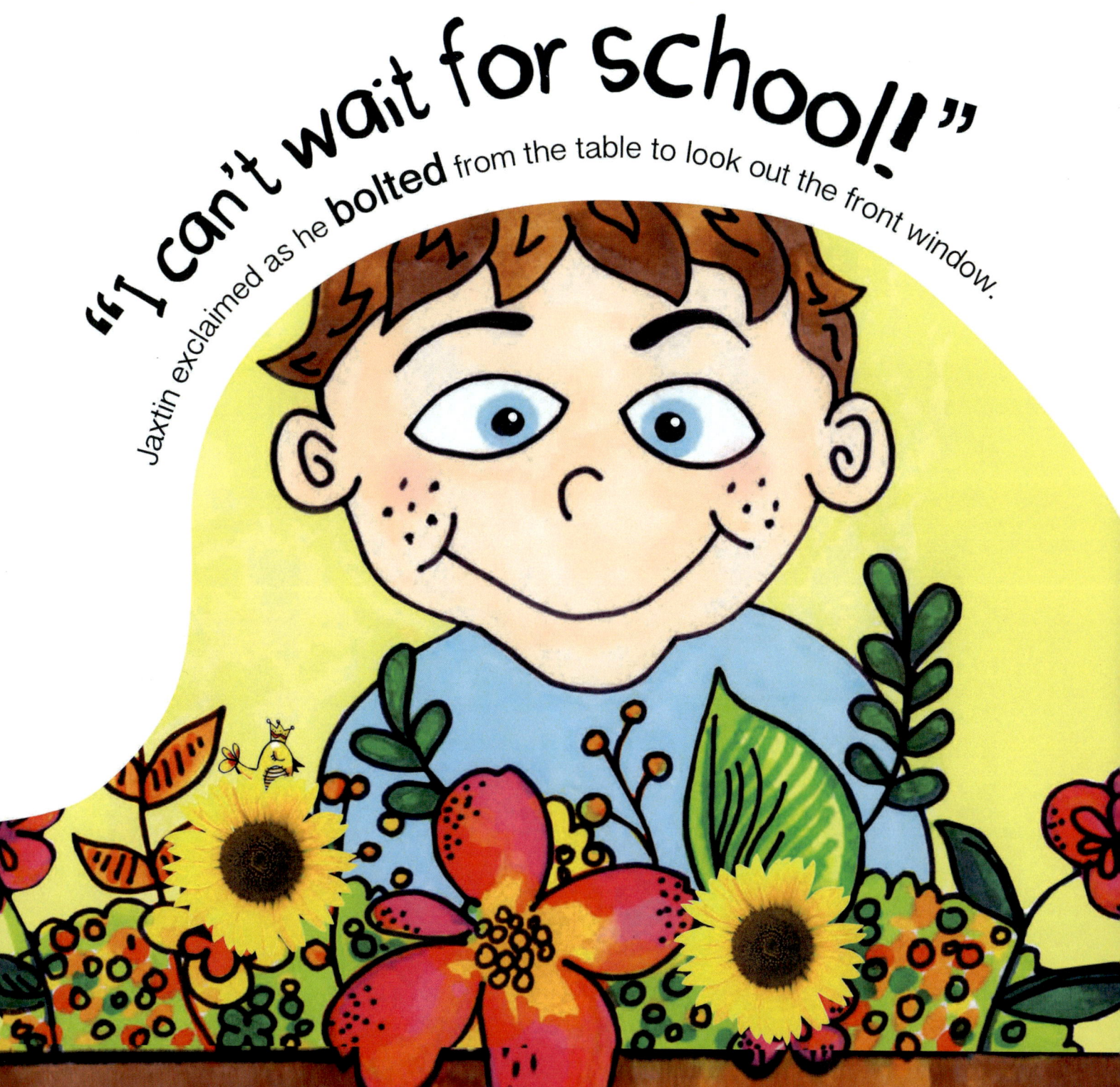

"I can't wait for school!" Jaxtin exclaimed as he **bolted** from the table to look out the front window.

Makayla, on the other hand, was **not** feeling his excitement. She was **nervous** about going to a new school.

"What if I don't make **any** new friends? What if the bullies make fun of me?"
"Will my teacher be as nice as Mrs. Rose was in second grade?"

"Will I even like third grade?!!"

"It's here!!!"

Jaxtin exclaimed as he grabbed **his half-zipped backpack** and headed out the door to the bus.

And there it was. Right there. Right in front of the driveway.

Makayla imagined the school bus as a **giant yellow submarine**, waiting to capture the children and take them to a castle dungeon, where they would meet a **dragon**.

At least Makayla had her magic necklace on. Her mom gave it to her as a reminder to always **be herself**. She told Makayla it would help her find her **inner magic.** Makayla would be able to use it, along with her imagination, to turn any negative feelings into positive ones.

"Just be yourself when the world gets tough and remember the inner magic inside of you," her mother said. "When a bully gets you down, don't leave with a frown. Be happy with just the way you are!"

Makayla tightened her hands around her necklace, took a deep breath, and stepped onto the big yellow submarine.

Just be yourself!

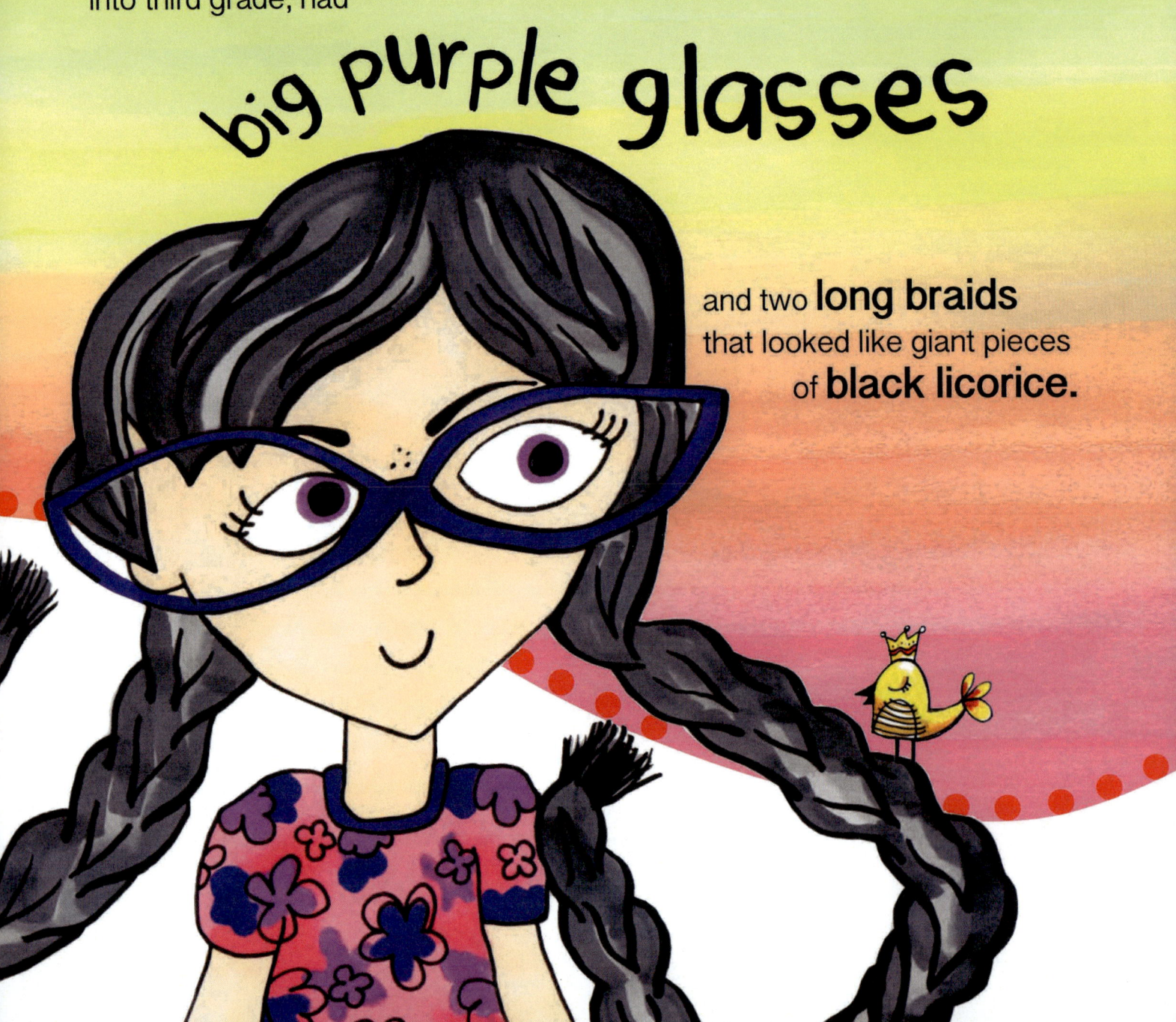

There were many types of **creatures** on the bus. Gracie, who was going into third grade, had **big purple glasses** and two **long braids** that looked like giant pieces of **black licorice.**

Daniel, a second grader, had a long tongue and shiny pebble eyes. He looked like a **big** giant lizard waiting to pounce.

Makayla did not see Jaxtin. She figured he must already be captured and on his way to face the dragon.

At last we arrived!!

"We're here!" yelled a voice behind Makayla. It was Jaxtin. He had been hiding in the back of the bus the whole time!

The school looked like a **giant castle** with marshmallow clouds reaching to the top.

"Remember what Mom says, Jaxtin, and just be yourself," Makayla said.

She grabbed Jaxtin's hand, took a deep breath and headed toward the entrance.

The classroom was busy, with more creatures than ever before.
Ms. Alyssa, Makayla's new teacher, was busy getting ready for the class's first activity.
She asked the students to draw a **sea creature** that reminded them of themselves.

"Attention class!!"

said Ms. Alyssa.

"It's time to present your work."

Since Makayla was a good swimmer, she decided to draw a fish.

"Nice picture! You look like a fish with big eyes!!"

The voice came from John, a dark-haired boy with **big, round glasses**.

Makayla took a deep breath, closed her eyes and held onto her necklace.

and live happily being just ME!

You silly bully, I will imagine and see all of the good things about me! So run along, far far along.

You cannot defeat the inner magic inside me!"

"Time for lunch!!"

exclaimed Ms. Alyssa. Makayla grabbed her favorite butterfly lunch box and headed to the lunch room.

"Chocolate pudding, my favorite!"

And then it happened. She **spilled** all over her new shirt. She was a complete **disaster!**

Before she could hide her mess, Colleen, the most popular girl in fourth grade, saw the big brown goo.

"You look like a little pink piggy!!"

she chuckled.

Makayla took a deep breath, closed her eyes and held onto her necklace.

"If I were a pig I could play in the mud and get dirty very often," Makayla thought. "I could make many friends like chickens and hens ...

That afternoon, Ms. Alyssa asked the students to write a short story about one of their **favorite summer adventures** to share with the class.

"It's story time!!"
said Ms. Alyssa.

It was Makayla's turn.

Her last chance to leave a **good impression.**

Since she loved animals, Makayla chose to tell a story about her trip to the **circus** this summer.

Before she could say more than a word, two tiny voices behind her whispered,

"You should be in the circus! I mean with those big ears, you might as well be an elephant!!"

It was Susan and Beth, **two sisters** who just moved to town a few months ago.

Makayla took a deep breath, closed her eyes and held onto her necklace.

She was almost there when the absolute, most horrible, unimaginable thing happened!

She tripped!

papers flew everywhere!!

They looked like an angry tornado of bees circling around her.

Suddenly, Makayla heard someone behind her. It was probably another bully, but she was ready. Holding onto her necklace, **slowly, she turned around**...

It was Ms. Alyssa!!

She had a soft smile with something shiny and glowing bright in her hand.

"This is for you, my **little hero**," she said softly as she handed Makayla a tiny treasure.

"Today you have proven that you are a **hero of kindness, love and inner magic**. I have seen you use your imagination to be yourself and turn negative feelings into positive ones. I'm giving you this new necklace to use as you go out into the world and help others see their own inner magic. You can help others see that they are magnificent just the way they are!"

"You are a true hero!"

On the way home, Makayla could hardly wait to share her news with her mom.

Her mom was waiting by the front door when Makayla and Jaxtin arrived. **"How did it go?"** she asked with excitement.

Makayla told her mom about her big surprise with tears of joy in her eyes, and said,

"Being just me is so awesome!!!

And I plan on keeping it that way!"

To all of the little monkeys out in the world, "Just be yourself when the world gets tough and remember the inner magic inside of you," her mother said. "When a bully gets you down, don't leave with a frown. Be happy with just the way you are!"

Made in the USA
Lexington, KY
24 March 2018